BEFORE USING...

 Before using this book, please read the guidelines inside the back cover. For a free copy of the detailed guidelines go to www.hunterhouse.com or call the ordering number below.

🖉 To prevent bleed-through, it is recommended that water-based, rather than spirit-based, markers or pens be used in this Workbook.

NO MORE HURT

A Hunter House Growth and Recovery Workbook
by Wendy Deaton, M.A., M.F.C.C.
and Kendall Johnson, Ph.D.

ISBN-10: 0-89793-083-5   ISBN-13: 978-0-89793-083-3

ORDERING INFORMATION

Additional copies of this and other Growth and Recovery Workbooks may be obtained from Hunter House. Bulk discounts are available for professional offices and recognized organizations.

All single workbooks: $11.95

THE GROWTH AND RECOVERY WORKBOOKS (GROW) SERIES

A creative, child-friendly program designed for use with elementary-school children, filled with original exercises to foster healing, self-understanding, and optimal growth.

Workbooks for children ages 9–12 include:

No More Hurt—provides a safe place for children who have been physically or sexually abused to explore and share their feelings

Living with My Family—helps children traumatized by domestic violence and family fights to identify and express their fears

Someone I Love Died—for children who have lost a loved one and who are dealing with grief, loss, and helplessness

A Separation in My Family—for children whose parents are separating or have already separated or divorced

Drinking and Drugs in My Family—for children who have family members who engage in regular alcohol and substance abuse

I Am a Survivor—for children who have survived an accident or fire, or a natural disaster such as a flood, hurricane, or earthquake

I Saw It Happen—for children who have witnessed a traumatic event such as a shooting at school, a frightening accident, or other violence

Workbooks for children ages 6–10 include:

My Own Thoughts and Feelings (for Girls); My Own Thoughts and Feelings (for Boys)—for exploring suspected trauma and early symptoms of depression, low self-esteem, family conflict, maladjustment, and nonspecific dysfunction

My Own Thoughts on Stopping the Hurt—for exploring suspected trauma and communicating with young children who may have suffered physical or sexual abuse

We welcome suggestions for new and needed workbooks

DISCLAIMER

This book is intended as a treatment tool for use in a therapeutic setting. It is not intended to be utilized for diagnostic or investigative purposes. It is not designed for and should not be recommended or suggested for use in any unsupervised or self-help or self-therapy setting, group, or situation whatsoever. Any professionals who use this book are exercising their own professional judgment and take full responsibility for doing so.

You are a very special person.
There is no one exactly like you in
the world.

Draw a picture of yourself here
and write your name in a special way.

Write five things that you like about yourself.

Write or draw a picture that tells about your family or where you live.

In every person's life some good things happen and some bad things happen. Here is a list of good things that can happen.

- [ ] having a new baby in the family
- [ ] having parents you love
- [ ] getting a pet
- [ ] being healthy
- [ ] getting good grades
- [ ] having a good friend

Check all the good things that have happened to you.

Write the other good things that have happened to you here.

_____

_____

_____

_____

4

Here is a list of bad things that can happen.

☐ a car accident
☐ a family that fights
☐ someone in the family is sick
☐ someone in the family dies
☐ a child is hurt by a grownup

Check the bad things that have happened to you.

Write the other bad things that have happened to you.

_____

_____

_____

_____

Two bad things that can happen to children are physical abuse and sexual abuse.

Physical abuse is when someone hurts a child by hitting, biting, burning, or in some other way.

Sexual abuse is when a grownup or someone a lot older touches or hurts a child in his or her private places.

NO ONE SHOULD HURT A CHILD.

Here are some things children say
they feel when they are hurt on
purpose by a grownup:

- ashamed
- sad
- angry
- hurt
- scared
- feel like hiding
- feel like running away
- feel like screaming
- feel like hurting someone else

Have you felt any of these feelings?

Write some other feelings you have
felt when someone hurt you.

_____

_____

_____

_____

When you remember bad things that happened to you, you may not feel good. You may wish you could forget everything and never think about it again.

Write or draw a picture to tell what you wish would happen to bad memories.

Sometimes it is hard to remember
everything you saw or everything
that happened to you.

This list may help you remember some
of those things.

- a park
- hands
- a man
- a stranger
- a bathroom
- crying
- a fist
- a woman
- a face
- a bedroom
- a car
- a van
- slapping
- someone you know
- yelling
- bad names
- pictures

Others:

_____

_____

_____

Draw a picture of a really bad
thing that happened to you.

If you close your eyes and remember the __sounds__ of what happened, what did you hear?

Do you remember any smells?

Do you remember how your body felt?

Where were you when you got hurt?

_____

Draw a picture of that place.

Write how you feel about that place now.

_____

_____

_____

Do you feel safe in this place now?

_____

Are there other places where you
don't feel safe?

- school
- cars
- store
- park
- outside
- indoors
- your house
- another house

Where else?

_____

_____

Do some of these things
bother you now?

- being alone
- being in the dark
- meeting strangers
- sudden noises
- being outside
- being indoors
- riding on the freeway

Other:

_____

_____

Write how you feel
when these things happen.

_____

_____

_____

_____

Who have you told about
what happened?

_____

_____

Draw a picture of
how the person looked when
you told them what happened.

When a child is hurt
it may cause angry feelings.

Write or draw a picture to tell
about any angry feelings you have.

Write a letter to the person or persons who hurt you.

_____

_____

_____

_____

_____

_____

_____

_____

_____

_____

Draw a picture of the worst
thing you worry might happen to you.

Make a list of things that would help
you to feel safe.

Being hurt can give you bad dreams.

Write about or draw a picture of
any bad dreams you have had.

What do you do when you have
a bad dream?

_____

_____

_____

_____

_____

Write or draw a picture of a dream you would <u>like</u> to have.

Write some things you feel now about
being hurt.

_____

_____

_____

_____

_____

_____

_____

_____

_____

_____

Draw a picture of these feelings.

Draw a picture of you
before you were hurt.

Draw a picture of you now.

Make a list of people you can talk to about what happened and who you can talk to about other problems in the future.

_____

_____

_____

_____

_____

_____

_____

_____

_____

_____

Hope means you believe things can get better. Maybe things are not so good in your life right now, but someday they will be better. You can have hope.

Write a story about hope (you can draw pictures if you like).

If you were in a race what kind of race would it be?

- [ ] skates
- [ ] running
- [ ] cars
- [ ] swimming
- [ ] skis
- [ ] skateboard
- [ ] bike
- [ ] sleds

What else?

_____

_____

If you were in a game or sport what would it be?

- [ ] volleyball
- [ ] soccer
- [ ] baseball
- [ ] hockey
- [ ] tennis
- [ ] softball
- [ ] football

What else?

_____

_____

What are the things you need to win in games and anywhere else?

- understanding
- luck
- speed
- practice
- strength
- friends

What else?

_____

_____

These are the same things that can help you be a winner now!

Draw a big poster that tells people not to hurt children.

Make a list of five good things in your life right now.

Write three wishes you have for the future.

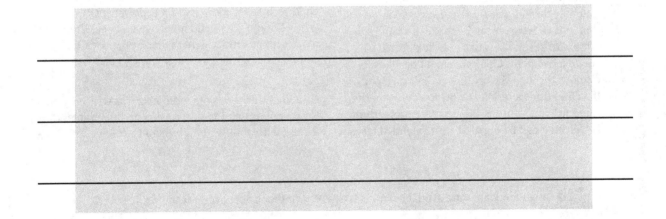

PLEASE READ THIS...

This is a brief guide to the design and use of the Growth and Recovery (GROW) workbooks from Hunter House. It is excerpted from detailed guidelines that can be downloaded from www.hunterhouse.com or are available free through the mail by calling the ordering number at the bottom of the page. Please consult the detailed guidelines before using this workbook for the first time.

GROW workbooks provide a way to open up communication with children who are not able to or who are reluctant to talk about a traumatic experience. They are not self-help books and are not designed for guardians or parents to use on their own with children. They address sensitive issues, and a child's recovery and healing require the safety, structured approach, and insight provided by a trained professional.

Each therapist will bring her own originality, creativity, and experience to the interaction and may adapt the tasks and activities in the workbooks, using other materials and activities. With less verbally oriented children, the use of art therapy or music or video may be recommended, or certain exercises may be conducted in groups.

Each pair of facing pages in the workbook provides the focus for a therapeutic "movement" that may take up one session. However, more than one movement can be made in a single session or several sessions may be devoted to a single movement. Children should be allowed to move through the process at their own pace. If a child finds a task too "hot" to approach, the therapist can return to it later. When something is fruitful it can be pursued with extended tasks.

While a therapist is free to select the order of activities for each child, the exercises are laid out in a progression based on the principles of critical incident stress management:

- initial exercises focus on building the therapeutic alliance
- the child is then led to relate an overview of the experience
- this is deepened by a "sensory-unpacking" designed to access and recover traumatic memories
- family experiences and changed living conditions, if any, are explored
- emotions are encouraged, explored, and validated.
- delayed reactions are dealt with, and resources are explored.
- the experience is integrated into the child's life through a series of strength-building exercises.

Specific pages in the GROW workbooks are cross-referenced to Dr. Kendall Johnson's book *Trauma in the Lives of Children* (Hunter House, Alameda, 1998). This provides additional information on the treatment of traumatized children.

The content of the workbooks should be shared with parents or significant adults only when the child feels ready for it and if it is therapeutically wise. Workbooks should not be given to children to take home until the therapeutic process is completed according to the therapist's satisfaction.

Although this series of workbooks was written for school-age children, the tasks are adaptable for use with younger children and adolescents.

Detailed guidelines are available for each GROW workbook (see list on front inside cover).

Printed in the USA
CPSIA information can be obtained
at www.ICGtesting.com
JSHW060145060224
56706JS00016B/885